Easy Solos

Vol. 2

For

Clarinet - 3212
Trumpet - 3803
Tenor Sax - 4202

I AIN'T GONNA STUDY WAR NO MORE

CLARINET
3212

TRUMPET
3803

TENOR SAX
4202

Traditional

2

THE SIDEWALKS OF NEW YORK

Charles B. Lawlor

CRADLE SONG

Johannes Brahms

ON TOP OF OLD SMOKY

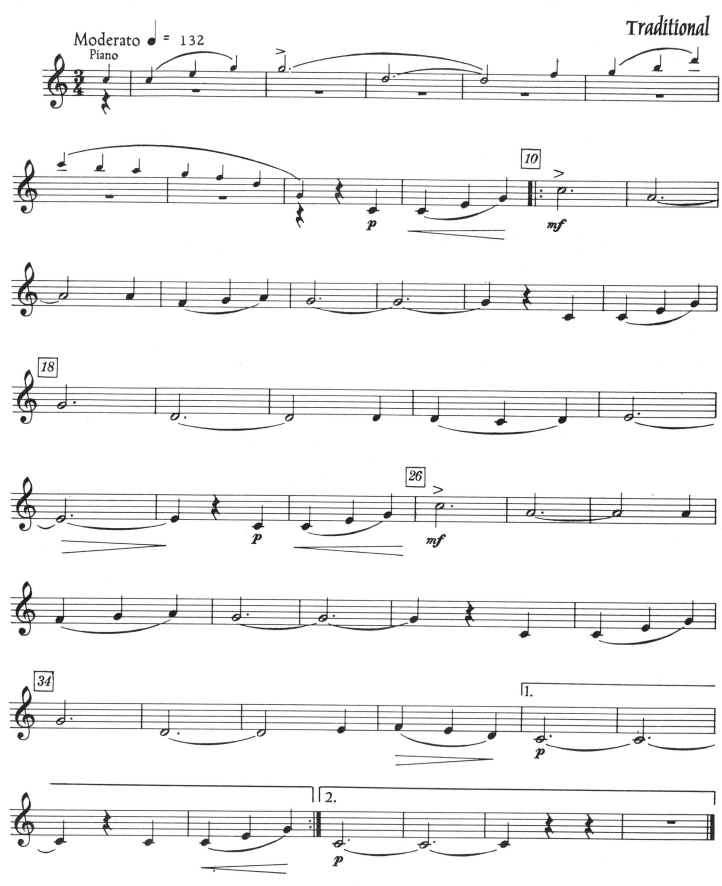

MR. FROG WENT A-COURTING

4 taps (2 meas.)
precede music.

Medium tempo ♩ = 88

Traditional

WHEN I WAS SINGLE

5 taps plus 1 silent beat
(2 meas.) precede music.

Bright tempo ♩ = 200

Traditional

FIREPROOF POLKA

Joseph Strauss

OLD PAINT

Moderately ♩ = 132

GREENSLEEVES

5 taps plus 1 silent beat
(2 meas.) precede music. ♩ = 120

Folk Song

YOU TELL ME YOUR DREAM

6 taps (2 meas.)
precede music.

Charles N. Daniels

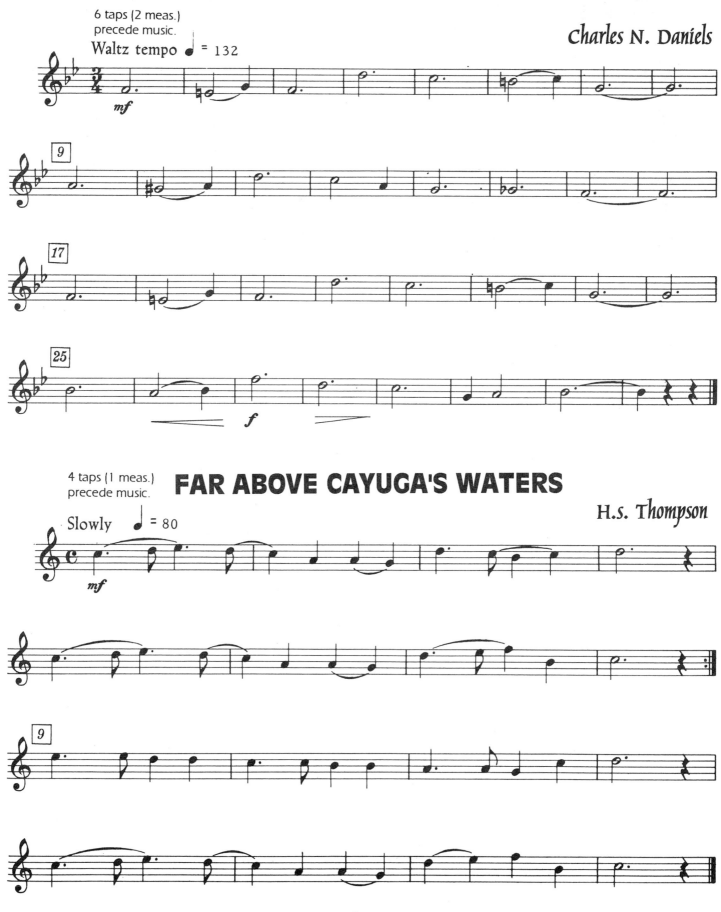

FAR ABOVE CAYUGA'S WATERS

4 taps (1 meas.)
precede music.

H.s. Thompson

SPANISH GUITAR

CARELESS LOVE

WHEN THE SAINTS GO MARCHING IN

LITTLE BROWN JUG

BLUES IN E-FLAT

Jay Arnold

HELLO! MA BABY

BLACK IS THE COLOR OF MY TRUE LOVE'S HAIR

15

JESU, JOY OF MAN'S DESIRING

H. M. S. PINAFORE

Sir Arthur Sullivan

PETER AND THE WOLF

THE HIGH SCHOOL CADETS

MANHATTAN BEACH

John Philip Sousa

4 taps (1 meas.)
precede music.

Trio

THE RIFLE REGIMENT

THE COSSACK

Traditional Russian Melody

RECRUITING SONG

from "GYPSY BARON"

Johann Strauss

THEME FROM "MOLDAU"

Bedrich Smetana

MELODY FROM "PRINCE IGOR"

Alexander Borodin

THE YOUNG PRINCE AND THE YOUNG PRINCESS

N. Rimsky-Korsakoff

SCENE FROM "BLUEBEARD"

26

SHEHERAZADE

from "ALBUM FOR THE YOUNG"

Robert Schumann

4 taps (1 meas.) precede music.
Poco lento ♩ = 80

THE STARS AND STRIPES FOREVER

John Philip Sousa

TOREADOR SONG
from "CARMEN"

G. Bizet

BERCEUSE
from "L'OISEAU DE FEU"

Igor Stravinsky

NOCTURNE

5 taps (1⅔ meas.)
precede music.

Andante tranquillo ♩ = 72

Felix Mendelssohn

poco ritard.

MODERATO CON MOTO

from 'CLARINET SONATA, Op. 120"

Johannes Brahms

VALSE NOBLE

Franz Schubert

IN DULCI JUBILO

5 taps plus 1 silent beat
(2 meas.) precede music.

Moderato ♩ = 96

J.S. Bach

mf

rit.

a tempo

p

mf

rit.

4 taps (1 meas.)
precede music.

CHORALE No.83

J.S. Bach

Moderato ♩ = 69

mf

rit.